BRITAIN IN OLD PHOTOGRAPHS

BARNES, MORTLAKE AND SHEEN

PATRICK LOOBEY

ALAN SUTTON PUBLISHING LIMITED

Alan Sutton Publishing Limited
Phoenix Mill · Far Thrupp · Stroud
Gloucestershire · GL5 2BU

First published 1995

Copyright © Patrick Loobey, 1995

Cover photographs: front: The Bull public
house, East Sheen, c. 1911; back: Barnes High
Street, c. 1904.

British Library Cataloguing in Publication Data
A catalogue record for this book is available from
the British Library.

ISBN 0–7509–0723–1

Typeset in 9/10 Sabon.
Typesetting and origination by
Alan Sutton Publishing Limited.
Printed in Great Britain by
Ebenezer Baylis, Worcester.

Patrick Loobey was born in 1947 and has lived in Balham, Putney, Southfields and Streatham – all within the Borough of Wandsworth. In 1969 he joined the Wandsworth Historical Society (founded in 1953) and has served on its archaeological, publishing and management committees. He was chairman of the society from 1991 to 1994. He has a wide-ranging collection of approximately 20,000 Edwardian postcards of Wandsworth Borough and south-west London, encompassing many local roads and subjects.

The captions to the photographs in this book offer but a brief glimpse into the varied and complex history of the area. For those seeking further information, the Barnes and Mortlake History Society, founded in 1955, have published booklets on the history of the area and hold meetings at the Sheen Centre, Sheen Lane. Street Names of Barnes, Mortlake and East Sheen, Raymond C. Gill (1977) is also a helpful reference book. The staff at the Local Studies Library at Richmond are most helpful with enquiries, and the library holds early newspapers, deeds, directories, maps and parish records, which are all available to those wishing to research names, dates and addresses of families or business concerns.

I sincerely miss the late Charles Hailstone and his keen love of local history. His knowledge of Barnes was revealed in the publication Highways and Byways of Barnes (1992), and recollections of the many conversations we had remain impressed on my memory.

All measurements within these pages are in Imperial and prices given in pounds, shillings and pence (£ s. d.).

Reproductions of all of the views in this book are available from P.J. Loobey, 231 Mitcham Lane, Streatham, London, SW16 6PY (0181-769-0072).

Contents

The Bull's Head Hotel, Lonsdale Road, Barnes, *c.* 1914.

Introduction

The photographs reproduced within these pages illustrate well the changes that have occurred in the Barnes and Mortlake area since the end of Queen Victoria's reign at the beginning of the twentieth century.

Barnes and Mortlake had been isolated for centuries within the loop of the River Thames until 1827 when Hammersmith Bridge was built. With the bridge came the accompanying approach roads, which in the 1850s and subsequent years were gradually filled with housing. Many eighteenth-century mansions, the country houses of city gents and titled families, survived into the twentieth century, sadly only to be demolished as further housing developments encroached on the area, in particular during the period 1905 to 1915. Fortunately, the riverside at Barnes was saved from such development because of the reservoirs lying either side of Hammersmith Bridge, which are now being carefully converted into playing fields and bird sanctuaries.

The coming of the railway in 1846 was another incentive to the developers, who, after the 1880s, turned their hand to the shopping areas in Sheen Lane and Church Road, Barnes.

East Sheen was at one time exactly that, for Shene was the old name of the village that Henry VII renamed Richmond in 1501 to remind him of his beloved Richmond in Yorkshire. The palace at Shene was originally built by Edward III. The habit of using Sheen for East Sheen is strictly speaking incorrect, as this is usurping Richmond's former name, but I have preferred to follow popular practice in choosing a title for this book.

Mortlake, for several centuries the seat of the local manorial system, has had more of an industrial history than Barnes or East Sheen. The brewery on the riverside has been enlarged many times, requiring the demolition of many properties. The 1930s and 1960s saw many changes and the narrow High Street is now, in part, a four-lane dual carriageway.

The little lanes and alleyways in Barnes and around Christchurch in East Sheen are worth a visit to discover just what has survived from the original small riverside villages.

These photographs will assist those who seek to find out about the history and architecture of the area, bearing in mind the constant changes brought about by ever-evolving social and commercial requirements, and I hope that the book will bring back pleasant memories for those who perhaps remember the area before some of those changes took place.

P.J. Loobey
October 1995

The Terrace on the riverside, Barnes, *c.* 1904.

Section One

CASTELNAU

*The Red Lion Hotel and public house at the head of Castelnau, c. 1914. The pub has
changed little except for the addition of a beer garden. Among the Huguenot protestants who
fled to England after the Edict of Nantes (17 October 1685) during the reign of Louis XIV
was the Boileau family whose ancestral home, near Nîmes in the south of France, was called
Castelnau de la Garde. (NB: Castelnau rhymes with 'raw' and not with 'cow'.)*

The Ranelagh Club entrance from Castelnau, alongside the Red Lion public house, *c*. 1914. The gateposts have now gone and the roadway is tarmacked to accommodate school coaches.

The Ranelagh Club, *c*. 1914. The house was originally named Barn Elms House and dated from 1694, with additions in 1771. It was taken over by the Ranelagh Club in 1884 when the club moved from its premises in Fulham. The lake and grounds were much admired by many until the club closed in 1939. The house was left derelict and finally destroyed by fire in 1954, the glow from the flames lighting up the sky over Barnes and Putney. The author, together with a large crowd of inquisitive onlookers, viewed the sad remains the following morning. The lake has been filled in and now forms part of the present sports playing fields and running track, organized by the local authorities.

The entrance to the Ranelagh Club, *c.* 1914. Many people recall horses and carriages passing through this gateway in Lower Richmond Road, Putney. The carriageway is now a pedestrian entrance to a council housing estate; it is also a rare survival, within a London suburb, of a strip of medieval agricultural land.

Castelnau, *c*. 1914. The Barnes Motor Garage on Lowther Parade, to the left, proudly proclaimed that it was 'Always open', a pledge difficult to find today. Taxis and cars were available for hire from Jordan Charles Williams' motor garage, on the right just beyond the Red Lion, which in 1995 is still a car showroom.

Castelnau, *c*. 1914. The road was laid out by the Hammersmith Bridge Co. in the years after 1827, when the bridge was erected. Starting at the bridge end, the houses were built in small groups by various developers and few are of a similar design. The trees in the gardens are still a pleasant aspect of this road. Between 1827 and 1896 Castelnau was called Bridge Road.

Derwent House, No. 72 Castelnau, *c.* 1910. This was the residence of Lady Harris in 1914.

St Osmund's Church, Castelnau, *c.* 1950. In the 1950s the congregation wanted to replace the old chapel and this is one of the original designs for the new catholic church proposed by the architects, Marshall and Archard. The three windows either side of the entrance were omitted but otherwise the building looks very much like this artist's impression. The foundation stone was laid on 17 July 1954.

Castelnau, *c.* 1912. The children on the right are standing in front of No. 128. The iron railings on the garden walls were removed during the Second World War to assist in the manufacture of munitions, and few of the wooden fences and gates have survived the ravages of time and the requirements of the motor car.

Nos 99 to 101 Castelnau in 1908 when the building was in use as the South West London College for Boys. Mr Ernest B. Burridge was headmaster.

Castelnau, *c.* 1914. The decorative stone gateposts have survived in better condition than the gates themselves, but some have been removed to accommodate larger vehicles. Two 'B' type buses appear to have little competition for road space. Hammersmith Bridge can just be seen in the distance.

The Bridge Hotel (left) and the Boileau Arms public house (right), Castelnau, 1904. The Boileau Arms has undergone some recent renamings: during the 1980s it was known as the Old Rangoon, and it is now known as the Garden House. Above the doorway the date '*c.* 1894' can be made out. The renaming means that the historical connection with local landowner Major Charles Boileau is no longer obvious. Major Boileau donated land and money for the building of Holy Trinity Church nearby. The Bridge Hotel at No. 204 has one of those magnificent gas lamps hanging over the doorway. Some of these were taken down when electric lighting became more available, and others were put into storage at the beginning of the Second World War to avoid damage; few were subsequently replaced.

Hammersmith Bridge in 1913, with only horse-drawn transport and light vehicles to contend with. The bridge now suffers from the volume of traffic passing over it. The original bridge of 1827 was designed by W. Tierney Clarke and was replaced in 1887 with the present structure to the designs of Sir Joseph Bazelgette, for the Metropolitan Board of Works. The bridge has featured in many films, but its worst moment came when an IRA bomb exploded on the bridge on Wednesday 28 March 1939, damaging the suspension chains.

Section Two

THAMES SIDE

Elm Bank Mansions, c. 1913. Elm Bank Mansions, comprising forty-five separate apartments, was built in 1896 in the grounds of Elm Bank House, which was demolished in 1904. The house on the corner of Elm Bank Gardens (on the far left of the photograph) has the obvious name of The Tower and originally stood in the grounds of Elm Bank House.

The Terrace, 1913. Elm Bank Mansions is on the right and Barnes railway bridge in the background.

The University Boat Race, shown here about 1912, has been rowed on this course between Putney and Mortlake since 1845. The footpath across the railway bridge was supposed to be closed on race days, yet here we see hundreds of spectators cheering on from the bridge parapet. Today the event attracts fewer crowds as a result of television coverage.

Barnes railway bridge, 1912. The bridge was opened in 1849 as part of a loop line to Hounslow. Between 1891 and 1895 the three curved spans presently in use were added alongside the original flat bed structure on the upstream side. The 1849 portion is now defunct.

The paddle steamer *Orchid* passing upstream in 1908 with a full complement of passengers.

Barnes railway bridge and The Terrace, *c.* 1919, with the recently built river wall. The gradual sinking of southern Britain and consequent rising tides meant that this wall had to be replaced in the 1970s with an even higher one of concrete that has spoilt the riverside views.

The Terrace, in a view facing east from near the White Hart public house, 1904. The horse-drawn vehicle on the left is carrying laundry, while the other vehicle contains what looks like either meat or vegetables. The eighteenth-century properties on the right survive today.

The Terrace and railway bridge, from near the High Street, 1919. The chimney beyond the bridge was that of the Barnes Urban District Council electrical power plant in Mortlake High Street. The power station buildings remain as offices and studios but the chimney has disappeared. Many local authorities had the foresight to supply electricity within their own area and some were not absorbed into the national system until after the Second World War.

The riverside at Barnes, *c.* 1919. The white painted verandas visible between the trees in both photographs belong to the White Hart public house. In the lower scene, of a similar date, Elm Bank Mansions stand on the left with, on the gatepost on the corner, a signpost pointing to St Michael's Church.

The Terrace at Barnes, with horse-drawn buses conveying their human cargo between Richmond and Hammersmith, 1904. The composer Gustav Holst (1874–1934) lived at No. 10, next to Cleveland Gardens, from 1908 to 1913. A blue plaque has been affixed to the house.

Green's Boathouse, c. 1919. The boathouse stood next to the railway bridge but on the Chiswick bank. It was operated by Thomas Green, a waterman 'by appointment to His Majesty' (probably Edward VII). Boats were built and stored on the premises.

The Bull's Head Hotel, 1904. First mentioned in 1672 as the King's Head, the hotel had been renamed the Bull's Head by 1748. Rebuilt in 1845 and added to in 1874, the pub was situated next to the town wharf which must have brought much of its trade. Young & Co., the Wandsworth brewers, now run it as a jazz pub, frequented by some renowned jazz musicians.

The Bull's Head and the aptly named Waterman's Arms, *c*. 1919. Lonsdale Road runs down the middle of this scene, and the High Street to the right of the Waterman's Arms. Notice the full title of the Bull's Head includes the word 'hotel' for it did indeed provide accommodation for guests. The Union flag is proudly displayed outside.

Castelnau Gardens, Arundel Terrace, *c*. 1933. These blocks of flats were built at a similar time to Riverview Gardens nearby (see overleaf) and are situated off Castelnau at the bridge end.

Riverview Gardens, *c*. 1914. These blocks of apartments facing the river were completed in 1913. The terrace gardens were well managed and planted with a variety of shrubs and flowers. Today they are given over mainly to grass.

Section Three

BARNES VILLAGE

Barnes village from the air, c. 1925. The central feature is the pond, with Station Road

running just below. Essex House is in the centre left, with the High Street on the extreme

left. Church Road leads up to the top of the view.

Barnes High Street, 1904. Mrs P. Elders owned the stationers and newsagents at No. 4, and Daniel Cray the dairy at No. 1. Charles Duck was a saddler at No. 2, with Joseph Burns, watchmaker, at No. 3. Many of these local trades, providing for local needs, have sadly disappeared from our suburban villages.

Barnes High Street, c. 1950. One major difference between this scene and the previous one is the clutter of all the street furniture required to govern the motorist.

The shop front of Arthur Spratt's fruiterers, at No. 129 Church Road, decorated for the coronation of George VI in 1937. The telephone number under Mr Spratt's shop sign is Riverside 1339; the familiar local call code-names were not converted into number-only codes until the 1960s.

Barnes High Street, *c.* 1935. The Green Cover Library on the right had 3,000 titles in stock for loan on payment of a small weekly amount. Many libraries like this were called penny libraries. Hoardings are in place on the left in preparation for the construction of Seaforth Lodge. (Compare this scene with the one below.)

Many of the wealthy families from the larger houses had their own transport and here we see a handsome coach and pair with liveried coachmen aboard in Barnes High Street, *c.* 1904. On the right is a wonderful display of pots, pans and watering-cans outside the premises of Evans W. Evans, oil and colour merchants. At this time only five or six basic colours of paint were available and 'color' merchants sold a variety of coloured powders, which could be mixed with the paint to produce different shades.

Seaforth Lodge is seen here shortly after completion in the late 1930s. This concrete and brick complex of apartments also has shops on the pavement frontage, including Norjon Radio Services, on the far side of the entrance, and Maude, a ladies hairdressers, on the nearside.

Harry Bailey's butchers shop, No. 21 High Street, c. 1906. This Christmas display of game and birds for sale advertises prices such as geese at 8 s., fowls at 2s. 9d., pheasants at 5s. 6d., turkeys at 10s., and hares at 3s. Besides being licensed to sell game, Mr Bailey also has a good display of fish for sale.

The High Street, 1904. The lady on the right appears to be admiring the display in the shop-window of E.B. Stevens, hosiers, or perhaps she is pondering what to purchase from J.M. Rabnott, stationers, next door. The pony and trap is standing in front of No. 62, Threlkeld House, which was demolished and Seaforth Lodge erected on the site.

The pond with the Sun Inn beyond, c. 1912. Charles Hurst, blacksmith, operated from the premises to the left of the inn. To the right, at No. 15, behind the trees, is the premises of the London and South Western Bank and at No. 19 is the surgery of James Abernathy, medical officer for Barnes District and also public vaccinator for Mortlake and Barnes Districts. To the far right of the photograph, in the water, chain railings supported by stumpy white posts can just be made out. These were used as a guide so that carts could be driven through the pond to refresh the horses, and also to expand the joints of the wooden wheels of the carts during dry weather.

Essex House, Station Road, *c.* 1913. This private house, dating from the 1850s, is one of only two survivors of several large houses that stood in the centre of the village around the pond.

Church Road, *c.* 1950. On the far left is the premises of W.S. Bond, undertakers, and next door the newsagents shop named as the Barnes Bookstores. The trees on the right lead from the pond, and fill out the green leading to The Crescent.

The High School for Young Girls, No. 45 Church Road, *c.* 1912. This was a convent school run by a French order of nuns. Mother Superior was Madame Duhamel. The house itself was called The Lawn. Next door at No. 37 was St Mary's College, day and boarding school for girls, with Mrs Newman as principal.

Canon Kitson stands by the greenhouse doorway in the Rectory gardens, *c.* 1912. At the turn of the century the canon was closely involved with appeals against proposed tramways within Barnes, and in 1901 he appeared before a Parliamentary Committee where the views of Castelnau residents were plain in their objections. Kitson was Chairman of the Barnes Schools Education Committee, which managed the several local schools. Kitson Road was named in memory of the canon.

The Rectory and St Mary's Parish Church, *c.* 1912. The oldest part of the church is the fifteenth-century tower built of brick in the English perpendicular style. An electrical fault led to a disastrous fire in June 1978; the nave, much of the internal fabric and monuments were destroyed. Subsequent archaeological investigation revealed much of the medieval fabric, some of which dated from the eleventh century. The church was subsequently rebuilt.

Church Road, in a view facing east, *c*. 1912. On the left is the dome of Byfield Hall, a dance hall that incorporated the Ideal Picture and Theatre Co. with seats for 500 patrons. Beyond Byfield Gardens are the oil stores of Walton, Hassell & Port. The dairy cart on the right (just this side of the awning) is standing outside John Morrisons' dairy at No. 70 with, next door, Charles Bridger's Luncheon and Tea Rooms.

Church Road, in a view taken from Castelnau, *c*. 1912. On the corner of Elm Grove Road was the London City & Midland Bank. Three doors further along Church Road, where the shop awning is drawn down, is No. 96, E.A. Medus & Co., stationers, post and telegraph offices. Theatre tickets and rail tickets for the London Brighton & South Coast Railway Co. could be purchased here, and a public telephone was also available.

Section Four

BARNES COMMON

The toll house on Barnes Common, c. 1930. Built on the parish boundary with Putney,

probably in the eighteenth century, the building was in use only as a gatekeeper's lodge and

tolls were neither charged nor taken. The lodge was refurbished and reroofed in 1994.

Barnes cemetery, *c.* 1908. With space around St Mary's Parish Church becoming scarce, a decision was taken in 1854 to enclose 2 acres of Barnes Common as a new burial ground. Strangely the ground chosen was on the Putney side of the boundary.

The mail coach *Vivid* crossing Barnes Common in 1911. At the turn of the century some millionaires, as a hobby, re-enacted the coach runs of the early nineteenth century and held yearly competitions such as the marathon taking place in this photograph. (See also page 102.)

A 'B' type open-top bus travelling along Rock's Lane across the common en route to Liverpool Street, *c.* 1913. Before the nineteenth century the common was at the centre of more than one dispute, mainly concerning the unlawful grazing of animals or the removal of excessive amounts of timber or gravel. The former waste lands of the manor are now managed by the council as a reserved open space for all to enjoy.

Looking south towards Mill Hill from Beverley brook, *c.* 1913.

A mother and her children wander across Barnes Common in 1912 with little fear for their safety. Holidays were rare in those days and many people would spend their free time walking or just relaxing on the common.

Cricket on the common, *c.* 1950. The game has been played on the Putney side of the common since at least 1800 when complaints were made of cricket balls constantly landing on the roadway, to the obstruction of passing traffic. The cricket pitch was moved across the common to its present position when Putney hospital was built in 1912. Nearby is the Cricketer public house.

The Railway Tavern, Upper Richmond Road, 1904. The tavern closely resembled the nearby railway station, and the original building probably dated from the 1840s to '50s. The drinking fountain on the right was installed as a refuelling stop for horse-drawn transport but sadly was removed before the Second World War.

The Railway Tavern was rebuilt and renamed the Railway Hotel between 1904 and 1912, when this photograph was taken. The tree line has increased since this time, when animals had only recently been removed from grazing the common. The pub was renamed the Red Rover until it was converted into a restaurant during the 1980s. Today the building stands empty, awaiting a new use.

Motor traffic passing the Railway Hotel, seen here about 1914, had increased to the extent that the crossroad was deemed to warrant a fixed duty point for the police. These points would be manned for as much as eighteen hours a day. In the background are two No. 33 buses about to pass each other en route from Liverpool Street to East Sheen, and vice versa.

The entrance to Barnes railway station, *c.* 1914. The railway from Nine Elms, Battersea, to Richmond was opened in July 1846 when this little halt was built. Perhaps because the station never became oversubscribed it has been little altered and is now the second oldest in Greater London.

Barnes railway station, 1971. The tracks were doubled from two to four lines in 1886 which necessitated the rebuilding of the road bridge. The signal-box was required here for diverting traffic on to the Hounslow loop line and for the sidings on the eastern side of Rocks Lane. This and the following photograph were taken by Charles Hailstone, a lifetime lover of local history until his unexpected death in May 1991.

Barnes railway station, 1971. Designed by Sir William Tite, the neo-Tudor design was to have 'tiled rather than a slate roof, chimney tops in character, and a small room in the roof'.

Mill Hill on Barnes Common, seen here about 1912, is the highest point in Barnes at almost 27 ft above ordnance datum. There are references to a mill in the area as early as 1443, and a post mill here was overturned in the hurricane of 1780. It was rebuilt as a smock mill and this survived until about 1836. Since then the site has been built over with a small group of individual private houses.

BEVERLEY BROOK
& BARNES POND

Beverley Brook, c. 1935. The brook runs along the bottom of the gardens of houses in
Willow Avenue, just visible through the trees on the left. The brook is probably named after
beavers that either lived along the banks or were bred nearby for their fur during the
medieval period.

Creek Bridge, Station Road, 1904. This is Beverley Path at the point where it becomes Willow Lane. The horse and cart are passing along Station Road heading towards Barnes village. The two-arched bridge was erected in 1792 at a total cost of £162 5s. 6d. To cope with modern traffic, the bridge has been replaced with a rather uninteresting but functional brick and concrete structure.

The rustic bridge crossing the Rythe near Ranelagh Avenue, 1904. The Rythe was a small tributary of Beverley Brook that drained off Putney lower common. Unpleasant odours came from what was no more than an open ditch so it was filled in shortly after this photograph was taken.

The upper view, taken about 1904, shows the earlier concrete weir on Beverley Brook, installed to improve the water flow. The lower scene includes the metal sluice gates which were erected by 1912, the date this photograph was taken. Water was led off at this point to feed the pond in the village centre. The United Reform church seen in the lower view was erected in 1906.

Station Road in June 1903. After several days of incessant rain Beverley Brook spilled over its banks and flooded a considerable area. Even the village pond was lost in a sea of water. The flooding was caused by development taking place further upstream in the Worcester Park and Raynes Park areas, which increased the amount of storm water run off into the Pyll Brook, a small tributary of Beverley Brook. A storm water relief culvert was eventually built along White Hart Lane in 1927.

Beverley Brook, *c.* 1912. Beverley Path leading into Willow Lane is in the distance.

Creek Bridge, Station Road, *c.* 1919. Willow Lane in the background suffered badly during the Second World War when a land mine exploded there. At the far end of the road was the premises of the Beverly Barnes Motor Works where 2½ to 5 litre luxury cars were built between 1924 and 1931.

Barnes pond, *c.* 1912. Few towns or villages near a major river have their own pond but Barnes is lucky to have a survivor of what was once a series of small ponds and moats in and near the village. The water was previously supplied from Beverley Brook but is now replenished with mains water.

Barnes pond, *c.* 1912. The water splash for horse carts had been removed by this time (see page 30). Children and artists are both drawn to this picturesque spot.

Barnes pond, 27 November 1904. Of the crowd of young boys on the ice only two have come prepared and are wearing skates while attempting a game of hockey.

Barnes Green School, *c.* 1912. The school was built in 1850 and later enlarged to accommodate 197 girls and 112 infants. In 1912 the average attendance was 169 girls and 98 infants. Miss E.J. Sewell was the headmistress, with a Miss Redway the infants' mistress.

Swans have always proved an attraction on the pond, as seen here about 1912, but during the 1980s intruders in the form of Canada geese have increased in alarming numbers to the detriment of our native species of wild fowl.

Section Six

BARNES STREETS

Ashleigh Road, c. 1919. In 1904 the properties listed were only Nos. 1 to 71 on the east side of the road and Nos. 2 to 20 on the west side. The road had grown considerably by 1914 with the numbers increased to 99 on the east and as far as 124 on the west side. Among the artisans living here in 1914 were Ernest Harris, watchmaker, at No. 7 and Frederick Mitchell, bootmaker, at No. 48. The Ashleigh School for Girls occupied the nearby Castelnau House until it was demolished in 1907.

Byfield Gardens, *c.* 1910. Although mainly a residential road, at No. 1a in 1914 was Gibbons & Co., builders, and also the furniture repository of Julian Wm. Goodwin. Edward Byfield, a governor of St Helena in the South Atlantic, lived his last years (he died in 1777) at Byfield House, a Georgian house demolished shortly before the road was built in 1904.

Clavering Avenue, *c.* 1912. These large houses surrounded by large blocks of flats have had some interesting residents such as, in 1914, at No. 34, Clarence Ham Sills MRCS, LRCP Lond., physician and surgeon.

Church Road, Barnes. These two scenes, dating from approximately 1912 and 1950, show an almost identical Sun Inn. The earlier view sports a speed limit sign of 10 m.p.h. The later view has traffic islands and the addition of stone pavements with kerb stones. Both retain the peaceful air of a rural village.

Cowley Road, *c.* 1912. Leading off Mortlake High Street and bounded by Worple Way North and the railway, this road probably received its name after Abraham Cowley (1618–67), the poet who resided for some years at Barn Elms.

Fitzgerald Avenue, *c.* 1912. Many local street names have an historical connection with former landowners and the Fitzgerald family possessed a considerable amount of land in Mortlake from the eighteenth century.

Glebe Road, *c.* 1910. Many private households had names on their properties and that on the right, by the post pillar box, is named Laverstock. Glebe land was a portion of land the rent for which was paid to the local church and parson as a means of augmenting church tithes.

Grange Road at a time of development in 1910. The Grange, seen on the left, dates from about 1730 and is now a home for the elderly run by the Richmond Housing Trust. The little girl by the green has a popular toy of the time, an iron hoop.

Hogger's Corner, *c.* 1908. Hogger's Corner was the name given to the row of four or five eighteenth-century houses shown in this photograph. It was actually part of the old Upper Richmond Road before it was straightened in 1930. In 1914 Samuel Hogger operated a wheelwrights and motor works at Nos 12–14, next door to the Market Gardener public house, in the middle of the row. It is now renamed the Maggot and Maybe. Further along the row is the Halfway House pub, which was rebuilt in the 1930s but retained its name. Just beyond this pub is Priest's Bridge, which has given its name to this whole section of road. One possible reason for this name is that before 1348, when Mortlake Church was built, the priest of Wimbledon took this route to visit his flock at Barnes and Mortlake.

Lonsdale Road, *c.* 1904. The earliest development of the 1830s and 1840s took place at this end of the road following the building of Hammersmith Bridge in 1827 and the laying out of Castelnau. The people on the cart are either collecting for the Red Cross or participating in a fête.

Barnes Bowling Club, Lonsdale Road, *c*. 1930. The green is near Gerrard's Road in the grounds of the Barnes Sports Club, founded in 1920, which today offers activities including hockey, squash, tennis, cricket, bowls, croquet and snooker.

Lonsdale Road, *c.* 1912. William Lowther, second Earl of Lonsdale, bought St Ann's on the Barnes river front and acquired a considerable amount of land in the area in the 1840s and '50s. This road was originally called Lower Bridge Road. St Ann's House and estate faced the river, on the site where Lonsdale Road has been built. The house itself stood at the western end of the road, where St Ann's Terrace was built (see opposite). St Ann's House had a large tower, which provided good views of the river.

St Ann's Terrace, Lonsdale Road, *c.* 1909. The terrace of late Victorian houses overlooks the Thames and provides a grandstand view of the University Boat Race. The trees on the left cover the 12½ acres of what had been known for almost 1,000 years as 'Putney detached', meadowland for cattle grazing belonging to Putney landholders who own 15 acres or more. Barnes Urban District Council only took final possession of this odd parcel of land in 1906.

Carmichael Court, on the corner of Terrace Gardens and The Grove at the rear of Malthouse Passage, *c.* 1935. This block of private apartments was partially erected on the site of Malthouse Cottages, themselves a conversion from an old malthouse, which were demolished in 1911.

Madrid Road, *c.* 1912. The name of the road reflects one of the many overseas postings of the landowner, the diplomat Sir Gerrard Augustus Lowther KCMG, CB, at the turn of the century.

Rosslyn Avenue in 1912, with recently planted trees struggling skywards. This is part of the small estate of houses nicknamed White City due to the similarity of its white stucco-fronted houses and the White City grounds in Shepherd's Bush, opened in 1908 for the Franco-British exhibition.

Station Road, where Creek Bridge crosses Beverley Brook. Willow Avenue is to the right. The slight hump in the old bridge is quite noticeable in this view.

Sutherland Gardens, *c*. 1912. The photograph is taken facing Grosvenor Gardens from the Upper Richmond Road.

An early photograph of Tudor Gardens, probably taken about 1912, before the permanent surface, pavement and kerbstones were laid. This is part of the White City estate which included Treen Avenue, Rosslyn Avenue and Priory Gardens.

Queen's Ride, Barnes Common, *c.* 1906. After Putney Bridge was opened in 1729, Queen Caroline, wife of George II, instigated improvements to this road, between 1736–40, to improve access to Richmond Park.

White Hart Lane, 1912. The level crossing is still in use but is now controlled automatically with accompanying flashing lights. The lane was the old boundary between Barnes and Mortlake.

White Hart Lane in 1912, with Railway Street on the right. The Cambridge Dairy is on the left with the confectioners shop of H. Wallis next door. Further along on the right, with the ornamental iron work on the roof, is the Edinburgh Castle public house on the corner of Archway Street.

White Hart Lane in 1912, with the White Hart public house at the far end of the road. On the left is the provision store of M. Jackson and further along the Rose Sanitary Laundry. Before the Second World War most households did not possess a washing machine, the copper sufficing for smaller families. Many women found employment in the laundries or supplemented their income by taking in washing.

The White Hart, *c.* 1890. A stone above the entrance, now lost, gave the founding date as 1622. The pub was called the King's Head until 1766, when it is first recorded as the White Hart. At the turn of the century it was substantially rebuilt, as seen in the photograph on the next page.

The White Hart, *c.* 1904. The London General Omnibus Company horse bus is awaiting passengers before plying the route to Castelnau.

White Hart Lane, *c.* 1914. The photograph shows the Thorne Terrace parade of shops on the corner of Archway Street, which runs off to the right. The well-stocked display of fruit and vegetables is outside E. Reed's shop. Next door is J. Fords, fishmonger, and finally the newsagents and tobacconists of H. Turvill. The newspaper banners mention men trapped in a South Wales coal mine disaster.

The Broadway shops on the corner of White Hart Lane and Mortlake High Street, *c.* 1912. They include the Broadway Meat Stores and the Broadway Dining Rooms. Brandons bottled beers could be yours for 2*s.* 6*d.* a dozen.

MORTLAKE

The parish church of St Mary, Mortlake, c. 1912. The first church was erected in 1348 when the people of Mortlake were given permission to purchase 9 perches of land, on the site where the large Watney Brewery was later built. The present church was resited in 1543 on the south side and east end of the High Street. Thomas Bouchier, Archbishop of Canterbury from 1454 to 1486, gave the font to the church in about 1465.

William's Lane, *c.* 1914. The River Thames can be seen at the end of the lane. The one property listed before the Second World War was Pink's Farm, occupied by George W. Stevens. The ramp for Chiswick Bridge overshadows the lane today.

Wigan's Lane, *c.* 1914. This lane was named after Sir Frederick Wigan, who in 1895 purchased a building near Mortlake station for use by local people as a parochial institute or village hall and which was named Wigan Hall (see page 122).

The Old Gateway in Cromwell Lane, *c.* 1906. These gates formed the front entrance to Cromwell House, a two-winged mansion dating from early Tudor times, probably built about 1485. The house was demolished in 1857, but the gates survive halfway along the lane. The Manor of Mortlake was taken over by Thomas Cromwell, Chancellor of the Exchequer and Secretary of State under Henry VIII. Cromwell, son of a Putney blacksmith, lost his head to the executioner in 1540, and the Manor of Mortlake was henceforth called the Manor of Wimbledon.

Two views of Mortlake Green, *c.* 1912. In a survey of the manor carried out in 1618 this was a 4-acre close (that is, an enclosed field) 'Lyeing south of the King's highway leadinge from Mortelake town toward Richmond and west of the highway leading from East Sheyme to Mortelake Street'. This became the village green, seen here with very neat and well-kept flower beds.

The Green and Sheen Lane, 1904. Before refrigerators were easily available, large quantities of ice were required in such concerns as public houses and fishmongers. The ice was normally covered in sacks and delivered on open carts, but a cold cabinet has been installed on the cart in this view.

The Green, with recently installed railings encompassing the new park, 1912. Oakeshotts Ltd, on the far corner at No. 2 Mortlake High Street, although listed as a grocers, was also a wine and spirit merchant and the window has a good display of those liquid products. The corner shops have since been demolished and replaced with offices. The Railway Tavern is more prominent now and the shops on the far side have also been replaced.

The Green, *c.* 1906. The parade of shops in Sheen Lane included Bird's Dairy, Herbert George Morris (printer), and Mrs Harritt Raggett's confectioners at No. 5. The Dining Rooms at No. 15, seen through the trees, were those of Charles Baker.

Sheen Lane, *c.* 1940. The Sheen Motor Spares on the left has for its shop sign an old-style motor tyre. At No. 11 is the Railway Tavern, a small eighteenth-century cottage converted into a beer house after the arrival of the railway.

The level crossing, Sheen Lane, *c.* 1904. The footbridge and station are on the right. Aldous & Son, drapers, at Nos 1 and 2 Station Buildings, has barely a square inch of space left in the windows because of the goods on display. The wooden crossing gates were replaced in 1975 and the signal-box was demolished when the signals were automated.

Mortlake railway station, Sheen Lane, *c.* 1914. The line was originally laid down by the Richmond Railway Co. and opened on Wednesday 22 July 1846. Trains were operated by the London and South Western Railway Co., which bought out the founder company in 1847.

Facilities at Mortlake station, seen here in 1914, included luggage porters and trolleys for moving large articles. There was also a well-stocked branch of W.H. Smith. The line's main income was generated from suburban traffic and, although sidings were installed at Barnes mainly as a coal depot, it was never intended for goods traffic.

First Avenue, c. 1924. An avenue of lime trees was removed in 1896 for construction of the road which was originally called The Avenue. When the adjoining road, Second Avenue, was constructed in 1905, this road was renamed First Avenue. (Once of those anomalies where second comes before first.) Half way along the road is Limes Field Road, leading through to White Hart Lane.

Second Avenue, *c.* 1912. Opposite this avenue, in the High Street, are the old house called The Limes and the fire station, which dates from 1904.

The riverside at Mortlake, *c.* 1912. Looking upstream at lowtide it is difficult to realize that this scene is within such close proximity to a city as vast as London.

Two views of the Chiswick foreshore, as seen from Mortlake, *c.* 1924. The railway bridge at Strand on the Green can be seen in the distance, but Chiswick road bridge was not added until 1932. An account from the year 1240 informs us that an enormous fish was chased up river for some miles and eventually speared and killed at Mortlake. The 'monster of monstrous' size is now thought to have been a whale.

The sailing barge *Alexander* from Faversham, probably delivering timber at Mortlake, *c.* 1914.

A crowded pleasure steamer travelling upstream passes Mortlake, *c.* 1924.

The brewery buildings of Watney & Co., seen here about 1904, are a prominent landmark. Over the centuries the brewery has swallowed up several riverside houses and streets. Thames Street, for example, was covered over in 1866, and the site of the manor house has also been built over. The brewery underwent some major rebuilding in the 1970s and is undergoing further alterations in 1995.

The brewery at Mortlake dates mainly from the Victorian era, when brewing companies were increasing their number of public houses to keep pace with development in London as a whole. The sailing barges and tug barges drawn up on the foreshore in these two views delivered the vast amounts of grain, hops, barley and coal required by the brewery. The Ship public house can be seen on the right of the lower view.

The sweep of the Thames from Mortlake towards Barnes, *c.* 1924. The beached boat was named *Freedom*; perhaps it was a reference to retirement or escape from the horrors of the First World War. The river has been a great highway into Buckinghamshire and Berkshire since the Neolithic period, and an early style of pottery from those times is known as Mortlake ware from some samples discovered in the river hereabouts.

The south side of Mortlake High Street, from the corner of Sheen Lane, *c.* 1904. The large sign on the right, at No. 4, is the butchers shop of Richmond and Wright. Next door, at No. 6, is Samuel Garside, wine and spirit merchant; perhaps the boys gathered outside are considering the purchase of some ginger beer. All of these shops disappeared during road widening and rebuilding schemes in the 1960s.

Mortlake High Street, facing west towards the brewery with the wall of St Mary's Parish Church on the left, *c.* 1940. Mrs Ida McLoughlin had the confectioners shop at No. 98 on the left. At the far end of the row, at Nos 80 to 86, with the furniture on the pavement outside, was the pawnbrokers of Felix McCabe & Sons. All of these properties beyond the parish church have been demolished and council housing blocks erected in their place.

Mortlake High Street, facing east, 1904. Edward March, in his apron, stands by the door of his butchers shop at No. 36. Further along is the Old George public house, demolished for road widening but rebuilt by Young & Co. as the Charlie Butler public house. At the time this photograph was taken, the width of road here was only about 12 feet.

The fire station at No. 121 High Street, 1904. The horse-drawn steam appliance is on a practice call out. Barnes Urban District Council used The Limes, on the left at No. 119, as council offices where the Chief Clerk, the Engineer and Surveyor, the Medical Officer of Health and the Sanitary Inspector could be contacted. The Limes survives today, as does the fire station built by Barnes UDC in 1904.

William Knight was the Station Officer at Barnes Fire Station in 1914, the approximate date of this view. Motor fire appliances had replaced the old horse-drawn engines by this time.

Mortlake High Street, facing west towards the brewery, *c.* 1914. The timber stack on the right is at the entrance to the premises of Eastwood & Co. Ltd, brickmakers, lime, cement and timber merchants. Further along is Miralite Ltd, art metal foundry. Tapestry House is the large building next to the Two Brewers public house, further along the road. Between 1619 and 1703 tapestries to the designs of Raphael were made at Mortlake, portions of which survive in the V & A Museum. The railings at No. 109, on the right, survive as do the eighteenth-century houses at Nos 103 and 101.

Mortlake High Street, 14 September 1932. Barnes Urban District Council was granted a charter giving it borough status on 29 August 1932. Here we see the celebration parade with military bands heading towards the council offices. In 1965 Barnes was incorporated into the London Borough of Richmond upon Thames.

A very early photograph of Mortlake High Street, facing west, *c.* 1867. The premises on the immediate left is No. 36, later to become Edward March's butchers (see page 81). The scene looks like a set from a Dickens novel, with a dusty gravel road and a lack of street lamps.

The Mortlake Convention, 18 June 1914. The clergy leading the procession are headed by the Revd Horace Granville Monroe, vicar of the parish church. F.H. Wootton, the shoeshop on the far left, is offering handsewn shoes or boots for gents at 18*s*. 6*d*. and for ladies at 16*s*. 6*d*.

The Mortlake Convention

The Mortlake Convention was a diocesan missionary convention held on 17, 18 and 19 June 1914. The meeting took place in a vast marquee in the grounds of The Cedars, East Sheen, where a crowd of 1,400 attended. The speakers included the Bishops of London, Southwark and Kingston. The procession marched from The Cedars along Sheen Lane, seen here, to the parish church on Thursday 18 June. The Cedars was a large eighteenth-century mansion, with gardens and extensive grounds, which stretched as far north as the Upper Richmond Road. It stood on the west side of Sheen Lane, near what is now Penrhyn Gardens. The house was the home of Edward Hugh and Arthur Leycester-Penrhyn, both local JPs.

A procession of military bands comes to a halt in Sheen Lane at the corner of Vernon Road some time before August 1907, when this postcard was posted.

Empire Day at the Mortlake National School, 24 May 1909. Queen Victoria's birthday was celebrated in all schools on Empire Day, when the Union flag was hoisted on the flag-pole watched by the children in their Sunday best. Among the hundreds of participants and onlookers here there is hardly a bare head in sight; the girls and women wear large brimmed hats and all of the boys and men wear either caps or hats. The school, now demolished, stood close to the parish church, near Mullin's Path and Vineyard Road.

The Jolly Milkman public house next to Mortlake Green and Cromwell Place in the Lower Richmond Road, photographed by Charles Hailstone on 2 October 1944. The pub has recently been renamed the Pickled Newt.

The Jolly Gardeners on the corner of Ship Lane, 2 October 1944. This is another photograph by Charles Hailstone, who may well have taken them because he was aware that important local buildings such as this could be lost during the V1 flying bomb raids taking place at that time. This pub is first recorded as the Three Tuns in 1720, and by its present name in 1796. The eighteenth-century building was demolished when it was deemed too small for modern trade and the present building was erected in 1922. Thankfully it retains its name.

EAST SHEEN

The Upper Richmond Road, East Sheen, c. 1914. The Hare and Hounds public house is on the left, in front of which is an open-top bus en route to Walham Green – now called Fulham Broadway.

The Upper Richmond Road, *c.* 1924. This parade of houses lies between Grosvenor Avenue and Grosvenor Gardens.

The private motor car was still a rarity when this view of the Upper Richmond Road was taken about 1914. Push carts and horse-drawn vehicles were used for deliveries well into the 1930s, and a few were still in use for the delivery of coal, bread or milk as late as the 1950s.

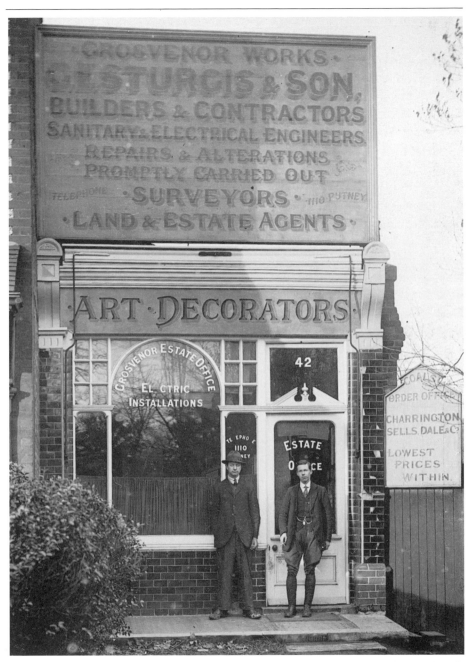

The offices of G.E. Sturgis & Son, No. 42 Upper Richmond Road, on the north side near Fitzgerald Avenue, *c.* 1920. The firm was a well-known local builders and contracters but it also acted as managing agents for several properties in Putney and Barnes.

The Upper Richmond Road at the junction with East Sheen Avenue, *c.* 1924. On the corner is Philip Davies Ltd, clothiers and drapers. Many of the following photographs were taken by R.J. Johns of Longley Road, Tooting, whose photography business was started in 1911 and continued up to about 1936, and who printed many of his scenes as picture postcards.

Troops on the march along the Upper Richmond Road, passing the junction of Portman Avenue, *c.* 1914.

The Hare and Hounds public house, *c.* 1912 (above) and *c.* 1935 (below). The pub dates from at least 1776 and was recorded then with that name. In the same year the nearby estate of Palewell was described as having a pack of hounds, perhaps the origin of the pub's name. Until the First World War stabling was available here.

The junction of Palewell Park with the Upper Richmond Road, *c*. 1924. On the left are the furniture showrooms of Bernard B. Trevax. Further on, with its goods spilling out on to the pavement, is Charles Henry Mitchell's china shop.

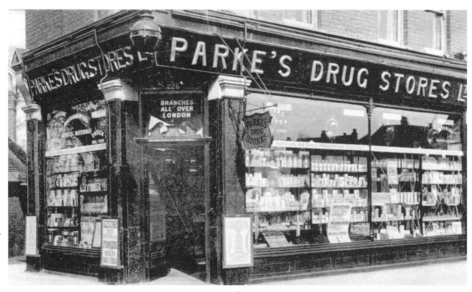

Parke's drug stores, No. 226 Upper Richmond Road, on the corner of Milton Road, *c*. 1912. With branches in Richmond and Putney, the firm sold a range of items from Kodak films and artists' materials to influenza mixture at a shilling a bottle. It was also willing to deliver prescriptions.

The shoeshop of W. Pearse, No. 220 Upper Richmond Road, 1910. During its 'Great Sale' prices ranged from 1*s*. 3*d*. to 8*s*. 11*d*.

John Perring's shop on the corner of Sheen Lane and the Upper Richmond Road, *c*. 1912. At this time, the shop was offering babies' push chairs at 6*s*. 11*d*. and 8*s*. 11*d*., with linoleum floor covering at 1*s*. 6*d*. and 2*s*. 9*d*. per yard. The aptly named Ivy Cottage on the right was demolished for road widening.

The date of this scene of the Upper Richmond Road must be between 1939 and 1944, more probably the early part of the war, as Maynard's newsagents is displaying placards announcing 'Balloon barrage foils raiders'. A bomb did fall nearby at the rear of the Bull public house in 1941, destroying a council building and blowing out windows of shop fronts in Sheen Lane. The raider in this instance was shot down by a Spitfire and crashed in the Thames at Richmond.

An almost identical view to the one on the previous page but in the more peaceful time of about 1950.

The crossroads at East Sheen, in a view facing east, *c.* 1924. Ivy Cottage has now gone and preparations are being made to erect the war memorial on the triangle of land on the right of the junction.

Compare this view of the crossroads, *c.* 1946, with that on the previous page. Notable additions are the police call box and the public toilets (the entrance to which can just be seen alongside the call box), for which Barnes Urban District Council had to borrow £3,000. Other changes include the installation of traffic lights and a new-look Bull public house, rebuilt in 1938. (The war memorial is hidden from view behind the building on the right.)

The war memorial to the 249 men of Barnes and Mortlake killed during the First World War. It is surrounded by many personal tributes of flowers from relatives and friends. The names of the men are recorded on a commemorative scroll, kept within a glass cylinder, which is situated beneath the sword of honour at the foot of the memorial. The memorial is seen here probably in November 1925, eight months after the unveiling ceremony carried out in April by Admiral A.M. Duff.

The Triangle in Sheen Lane, when it was still a small oasis of trees and bushes, *c.* 1912. On the extreme right is the Picture Drome, an early cinema in the area which opened on Boxing Day 1910. The milestone at one corner of The Triangle led to it being called Milestone Green.

A photograph taken in 1950, from almost exactly the same viewpoint as the one above. The Picture Drome was demolished in 1929 and replaced with the Odeon. The cinema opened as the Sheen on 22 December 1930 with the film *Hold Everything*. At one stage it was also called the Empire and was finally renamed the Odeon in 1944. It closed on 3 June 1961 and was subsequently demolished.

The Triangle, *c.* 1908 (above) and *c.* 1914 (below). In the lower photograph the No. 37 bus is en route from Herne Hill to Isleworth. Behind it is the Hornby Model Dairy, which kept its cows on Petersham meadows by the riverside. The Picture Drome is on the right, behind the trees.

Looking south over the crossroads towards the Odeon cinema, *c.* 1950. The impressive size of the building can be appreciated in this view. After the cinema was demolished a block of offices and showrooms was built on the site.

Looking north into Sheen Lane over the crossroads, *c.* 1940. Compare this view with those on the two previous pages.

The Bull public house, as rebuilt in 1938, is on the right in this photograph which dates from about 1950. Beyond the pub is the large BP petrol station. Both were demolished in 1987 and replaced by a supermarket. The long row of shops with accommodation above, on the left, was erected in 1932 by the Putney building firm Adamson & Co.

The mail coach *Vivid* on a re-enactment run from Hampton Court to London, outside the Bull at East Sheen, *c.* 1911. (See also page 36.)

Graemesdyke Avenue is to the right of this view of the Upper Richmond Road, *c.* 1935. No doubt the little dairy cart on the roadway is from the dairy in the scene below.

Delivery carts outside the Clifford dairy of Long & Pocock, on the corner of Clifford Avenue and the Upper Richmond Road, *c.* 1912. This photograph must have been taken in the summertime as the churns are covered with an insulation blanket to keep them cool. Because of the lack of refrigeration, deliveries to the larger households sometimes took place two or three times a day.

Sheen Lane, facing south, *c.* 1939. On the left is W.H. Dadds & Sons' shoeshop, with its well-stocked window display, and next door, with its display of vegetables encroaching on to the pavement, is the provisions shop Hook's Stores. The Bedford delivery van on the right belongs to Southern Railways.

Facing south along Sheen Lane, *c.* 1914. The imposing building on the left is No. 41, the London & South Western bank. Next door is Harry Croxon's stationers, then Mrs Woolfrey's refreshment rooms and Edwards and Marshall's bootmakers. Vernon Road is on the left, just beyond the horse and cart.

Sheen Lane, with St Leonard's Road on the left and Milton Road to the right, *c.* 1912. Edwards' stores on the right was a corn merchant. Many corn merchants went out of business during the First World War because horses, which were vital to their delivery service, were requisitioned by the army and taken to the front in France. The four-storey building at No. 40 on the left was occupied by Rayner Canham's drapery shop.

Carlton Road, facing Ormonde Road from the Upper Richmond Road, *c.* 1914. The ultimate dream of the motorist of today would be to find a street as empty as this.

The Plough public house, Christchurch Road, *c.* 1907. The village bobby, resplendent in his polished-buttoned uniform, poses for the cameraman. The cottages and pub have hardly altered to this day.

Spencer's Cottages, Christchurch Road, *c.* 1912. The cottages bear the name of the Spencer family who, in the eighteenth century, bought the title to Wimbledon Manor, formerly called Mortlake Manor. By the 1830s, however, the family was forced to sell off parcels of land because of financial problems, the British Land Co. being a major purchaser.

Christchurch, seen here about 1920, was built in 1863 with a dedication to Edward Penrhyn Esq., who for over thirty years had promoted good works within the parish. The church was completed in 1887 with the construction of the north aisle. The immediate area around the church is a rabbit warren of lanes and alleyways well worth visiting, but on foot or bicycle and not by motor car.

No. 1 Connaught Avenue (above) was caught on camera and reproduced as a picture postcard for the occupants in 1912. What better way to show visitors where you live? The houses in Connaught Avenue below are almost obscured by the swiftly growing trees.

The higher end of East Sheen Avenue, *c.* 1924 (above), and facing north towards the Upper Richmond Road, *c.* 1912 (below). The newly planted trees above contrast sharply with the darkening aspect of the mature planes below. The Medical Health Officer for Barnes, Mr Bertram Crossfield Stevens, lived at No. 6. He was also the superintendent for Barnes hospital.

The upper view of Coval Road shows the condition of the carriageway and pavement shortly after development began in 1910. At the far end, in the Upper Richmond Road, is an advertisement for the latest attraction at the Picture Drome, a film entitled *The Black Box*. The lower scene dates from about 1933, when Coval Lodge, built in the 1850s, was demolished in nearby Coval Gardens.

Fife Road, near East Sheen Gate, *c.* 1924. The road was named after a resident of East Sheen Lodge, the Duke of Fife, who received permission to block off a footpath that ran towards Stonehill Road. To compensate he provided the section of this road near East Sheen Gate.

Graemesdyke Avenue, viewed from the Upper Richmond Road, *c.* 1915.

Grosvenor Avenue, *c.* 1912. From 1931 to 1938 golf club manufacturers Cann and Taylor Ltd are listed as being at No. 37.

Leinster Avenue, seen here about 1915, takes its name from Leinster House, which stood on the north side of St Leonard's Road. The house was demolished in 1930 and Eastbourne Gardens was subsequently built on the site.

Martindale, *c.* 1914. This road connects Christchurch Road with Percival Road. The size of the trees in the background encourage the view that this area was recently quite rural.

Milton Road, *c.* 1924. The photograph shows the section of the road near the junction with Church Path, a well-worn route which led to St Mary's Parish Church in Mortlake. At the far end, fronting Sheen Lane, are Nelson's Cottages, erected in 1815.

Both these views of Palewell Park date from about 1912. The lady with the parasol is no doubt guarding her fair skin from any risk of a suntan. The name Palewell can be traced back to the sixteenth century, when it referred to a well on the common enclosed by a protective fence or pale.

Palmerston Road about 1912, two years after the name was approved by the council. The third Viscount Palmerston (1784–1865), Prime Minister in 1855 and 1859, inherited Temple Grove in East Sheen upon the death of the second Viscount in 1802, but he sold off the property soon afterwards.

Richmond Park Road, *c.* 1924. During the 1930s East Sheen had its own Montessori infants' school at No. 63 Richmond Park Road. Mrs F.M. Gillham was principal. On the west side of the road, next to No. 76, were the hard tennis courts of Sheen House. H. Mumms was the honorary secretary of the club.

Both these views of St Leonard's Road date from about 1924. The entrance to the St Leonard's works of the builder R.T. Hughes can be seen on the left in the scene below. Formerly named Hampton Road after the landowner, Mr Hampton, the road was renamed after St Leonard's in Shoreditch, the birthplace of a Mr Cockburn, who was residing at Richmond when he had the first four houses built here in 1851.

Sheen Gate Gardens, *c*. 1914. This short road leading from Sheen Lane to the Upper Richmond Road had some powerful residents in the 1930s: Lieutenant Colonel McCaskill, Brigader General Magnus Mowat CBE, TD, and Lieutenant Colonel E.P. Barry. One of four doctors' surgeries in the Chamberlain, Wallis & Fisher group was also in the road.

Vernon Road, *c*. 1914. The Congregational church was founded in 1662 and this church, now a United Reform church, was erected to commemorate the centenary of the Sunday school in 1907. Howgate and Keith were the architects of the church, which was almost art nouveau in style and had copper capping on the porch and the tower.

Two views of Vicarage Road, *c.* 1912–14. On the south side of the road is Mortlake House, built in 1867 as a vicarage for the vicar of Mortlake and East Sheen and used as such until it was sold in 1954. It is now a private residence.

Ladies, in their up-to-the-minute fashions, inspect one of the stalls at the country fair in July 1914. The event was held in the grounds of East Sheen Lodge, which was the home of the Duke and Duchess of Fife until 1906. The house was converted into flats, but demolished in 1965. The site is now covered by York Avenue and Hood Avenue at the upper end of Sheen Lane.

Palewell Common, *c*. 1950. Now a small park and playground with space for football to be played, the common is squeezed between Beverley Brook to the east, Richmond Park on the south and housing in East Sheen on the west.

Sheen Common, *c.* 1912. This is a small piece of common land not enclosed within Richmond Park and kept open with ready access for the public.

This small pond on Sheen Common, seen here about 1912, has attracted a crowd of small children.

The Sheen Gate entrance to Richmond Park, *c.* 1914. The notice on the right-hand gatepost warns that motor vehicles must not exceed 12 m.p.h.

The Sheen Gate entrance to Richmond Park, *c.* 1906 (above) and *c.* 1935 (below). Beyond the gate in the upper view is one of the lodges of Clare Lawn in Sheen Lane, the home of Lord and Lady Wigan. (See also page 68.)

The deer in Richmond Park, seen here about 1924, are a reminder of the reason Charles I enclosed the park in 1637, for use as a royal hunting ground. Approximately 800 fallow and red deer are given free range of the park today.

The White Lodge, seen here about 1924, was built about 1728 by George II as a retreat for members of the royal family, especially Queen Caroline. (See also page 62.) Viscount Sidmouth lived here from 1801 until his death in 1844. One of his visitors was Admiral Horatio Nelson, a few weeks before the battle of Trafalgar. The line of royal occupants is too long to list here, but mention should be made of the Prince of Wales, later King Edward VIII, who was born here on 23 June 1894. The Royal Ballet School has used the building since 1954.

Adam's pond and Sheen Lodge, Richmond Park, c. 1924. Originally a keeper's lodge situated to the east of Sheen Gate, the residence was granted to the Scottish Baron William Adam, Lord High Commissioner for Scotland, hence Adam's pond. From 1852 to 1892 Professor Sir Richard Owen, the first director of the Natural History Museum at South Kensington, lived here. The lodge was destroyed by German bombing during the Second World War.

The ponds within Richmond Park have always been a favourite spot for picnics and here a family is enjoying an outing in about 1924.

The South African hospital was erected just inside Richmond Gate during the First World War to help cope with the unprecedented numbers of wounded. The hospital remained in use during the rebuilding of the Star and Garter Home, for disabled ex-servicemen, on Richmond Hill after the war and was eventually demolished in 1925.

Priory Lane, *c.* 1912. The priory, an eighteenth-century house built in the Gothick style, became a nursing home in 1871. This lane, which leads to the Roehampton Gate of Richmond Park and passes the priory, was naturally given that name. The speed limit sign of 10 m.p.h. finishes with the words 'By order', but neglects to mention whose.

BRITAIN IN OLD PHOTOGRAPHS

To order any of these titles please telephone Littlehampton Book Services on 01903 721596